Lil Legends

First learning book of shapes

circle

wheel

oval

egg

triangle

sandwich

square

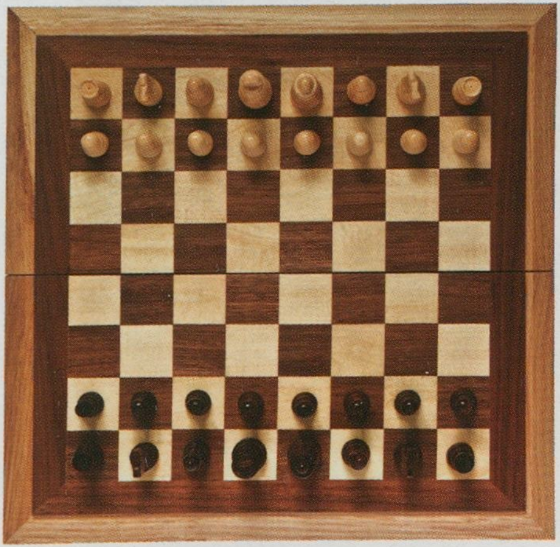

chess board

rectangle

envelope

rhombus

kite

star

starfish

pentagon

dog house

crescent

moon

heart

balloon

circle

oval

triangle

square

rectangle

rhombus

star

pentagon

crescent

heart

Lil Legends

VOTED PRODUCT OF THE YEAR
Consumer Survey of Product Innovation
2025

Designed for little hands and curious minds, Lil Legends Picture Board books are colourful treasures that foster observation and vocabulary skills in young learners. These beautifully crafted and sturdy books are invitations to explore, learn and grow. Open the pages and let the learning adventure begin!

* Winner Writing Books for Children Category.
Survey of 1800 people by NielsenIQ across categories.

Printed at Azure Press Pvt. Ltd., Bahadurgarh-124507, Haryana

Lil Legends
An imprint of
OSWAAL BOOKS

Head Office, Oswaal House
1/11, Sahitya Kunj, M.G. Road,
Agra (U.P.) India-282002
0562-2857671
contact@oswaalbooks.com
www.lillegendsbooks.com

ISBN
9 789359 580050

India	INR ₹	99.00
Abroad	USD $	5.00
	CAD $	6.00

Lil Legends
shapes